Mastering Python Package Managers: A Comprehensive Guide

To Become the Master of Dependency Management in your python project

Muthu Kumaran R

Table Of Contents

Table Of Contents

Introduction

    Why Python Package Managers Matter

    Overview of Python Package Management Landscape

Chapter 1: Getting Started with pip

    1.1 Installing pip

    1.2 Basic Usage of pip

    1.3 Managing Python Packages with pip

    1.4 Benefits

    1.5 Cons

    1.6 Uniqueness

Chapter 2: Virtual Environments: Packages Playground

    2.1 What Are Virtual Environments?

    2.2 Using venv (Python 3.3+)

    2.3 Using virtualenv (Python 2.x and 3.x)

    2.4 Isolating Project Dependencies

Chapter 3: Pipenv: Streamlining Project Management

    3.1 Introduction to Pipenv

    3.2 Installing and Setting Up Pipenv

    3.3 Creating and Managing Pipenv Projects

    3.4 Locking Dependency Versions

    3.5 Using Pipfile and Pipfile.lock

    3.6 Collaboration and Sharing Projects

    3.7 Pipenv for Development and Deployment

    3.8 Custom Scripts and More

Chapter 4: Poetry: Python Packaging with a Touch of Elegance

    4.1 Introducing Poetry

    4.2 Installing Poetry

    4.3 Managing Dependencies with Poetry

    4.4 Poetry Project and config Structure

    4.5 Poetry's pyproject.toml File

    4.6 Publishing Your Poetry

    4.7 Poetry in Action: An Example

Chapter 5: Conda: Managing Complex Environments and Beyond

    5.1 What is Conda?

    5.2 Installing Conda

    5.3 Managing Environments with Conda

    5.4 Managing Packages with Conda

    5.5 Exploring Conda Channels

5.6 Conda as a Universal Soldier

5.7 Conda Environments in Action: An Example

Chapter 6: Pixi: Where Python Packages Meet Pure Magic!

6.1 Hello Pixi !!

6.2 Pixi Installation

6.3 Pixi Project

6.4 Managing Pixi Package Dependencies

6.4 Pixi Configuration file Structure

Chapter 7: Advanced Package Management

7.1 Managing Multiple Python Versions with pyenv

7.2 Isolating Python Versions with Miniconda

7.3 Using Homebrew on macOS

7.4 Package Management on Linux Distributions

7.5 Managing Python-Based Command-Line Tools with pipx

7.6 Best Practices and Tips for Package Management

Chapter 8: Case Studies

8.1 Real-Time Case Studies

8.2 Data Science and Machine Learning with Anaconda

8.3 Web Development

8.4 Managing Cross-Platform Applications with Conda

8.5 Command-Line Tool Distribution with pipx

Chapter 9: Troubleshooting & Best Practices

9.1 Common Issues and Their Solutions

9.2 Ensuring Reproducible Environments

9.3 Security Considerations

9.4 Keeping Dependencies Up to Date

9.5 Cleaning Up and Managing Disk Space

Conclusion

Recap of Key Takeaways

Choosing the Right Tool for Your Projects

Embracing Best Practices

Future of Python Package Management

Your Journey as a Python Package Manager Master

Appendix A: Quick Reference Guides

Cheat Sheets for Pip, Pipenv, Poetry, Conda, and Other Tools

Glossary of Terms

Appendix B: Additional Resources

Recommended Books, Websites, and Forums

Advanced Topics for Further Learning

Introduction

Hello and welcome to the thrilling world of Python package managers! You've come to the perfect place if you're a Python enthusiast, a developer, or someone who simply enjoys writing Pythonic code (and maybe even wonders if Python could be the new secret sauce for world dominance).

In this book, we'll go deep into the Python ecosystem's often-overlooked superheroes: package managers. These unsung heroes are in charge of wrangling, distributing, and, dare I say it, "package-napping" all of the wonderful Python modules and tools you use in your projects.

Before you assume this book is about a lot of techie tools and terminology, let me tell you that we're going to make this journey as enjoyable, informative, and interesting as possible. After all, who said learning about software tools can't be a bit of a laugh?

Why Python Package Managers Matter

Imagine, for a moment, that you're planning to build a spaceship. Yes, a spaceship. Not your typical Python project, but bear with me. In this ambitious venture, you're going to need a lot of specialized parts and components, like warp engines, tractor beams, and a coffee machine that works in zero gravity (caffeine is essential for interstellar travel, after all).

In the world of Python, these spaceship components are the libraries and packages you need to bring your projects to life. Want to create a web app? You'll need FastAPI or Flask or Django. Dreaming of conquering the universe with machine learning? You'll want NumPy, Pandas, TensorFlow, and a sprinkle of scikit-learn. The list goes on, and it's as diverse as the aliens you might encounter on your cosmic voyage.

So, what does this have to do with Python package managers? Well, think of package managers as your personal fleet of starships. They help you locate, gather, and organize all those essential components. They make sure your warp engines don't conflict with your coffee machine and that your tractor beams don't accidentally tow a stray asteroid into your path.

In essence, package managers are the intergalactic traffic controllers of your Python projects. They ensure that everything runs smoothly, safely, and with just the right amount of quirkiness (because what's Python without a bit of whimsy?).

Overview of Python Package Management Landscape

Presently, you may ponder, "For what reason do we really want different package managers directors? Isn't one sufficient?" Well, it's a fair question. Python is a flexible language utilized in various spaces, from web improvement and data science to scientific computing and that's only the tip of the iceberg. Every one of these areas has its own unique necessities and challenges.

Imagine trying to build a zoo with just one type of animal. It might work for a while, but it's not going to satisfy everyone's taste for diversity. Similarly, the Python ecosystem is vast and diverse, and different package managers cater to different niches and scenarios.

In this book, we'll explore several Python package managers, each with its own strengths and quirks. We'll cover the ever-reliable `pip`, the project-centric `pipenv`, the modern `poetry` of package management, and even the cosmic powers of `Conda`. Each tool has its place in the Python galaxy, and we'll show you when and how to use them effectively.

So, buckle up, dear reader, as we embark on this epic journey through the Python package management cosmos. Get ready to discover the ins and outs of these tools, gain superpowers for your Python projects, and, most importantly, have a blast while doing it!

In the next chapter, we'll start our adventure with the trusty old friend of Python developers: `pip`. It's the package manager that's been with us since the dawn of Python time. So, grab your towel, and let's hitch a ride on the Pythonic express!

Chapter 1: Getting Started with pip

Welcome, fellow Python adventurers! In this chapter, we're going to kick things off by diving into the world of `pip`. No, not an enchanted word that makes things vanish; it's Python's trusty package manager.

1.1 Installing pip

So, you've decided to join the Python party, and the bouncer at the entryway is asking for your pip. No worries; we've got you covered. But first, a bit of Python humor: "Why is Voldemort so good with computers? He's fluent with Python!" □

To install `pip`, follow these simple steps:

1. **Check if you already have `pip`:**
   Open your terminal or command prompt and type below command to check the version of `pip`, if there is any.

```
pip --version
```

2. **Install `pip`:**
   ○ For Python 2.x, you might need to install `pip` separately. Try the following commands in your terminal or command prompt:

```
# for Linux, run below command in terminal
sudo apt-get install python-pip

# for Windows, run below command in command prompt
python -m ensurepip --default-pip
```

   ○ For Python 3.x, `pip` usually comes bundled with Python, so you should already have it. To check, type the following,

```
python3 -m pip --version
```

3. **Upgrade `pip` (Optional but recommended):**
   Even if you already have `pip`, it's a good idea to upgrade it to the latest version. Use the following command:

```
# for python 2.x, run below command
python -m pip install --upgrade pip

# for python 3.x, run below command
python3 -m pip install --upgrade pip

# if pip is in the SYSTEM PATH, run below command
pip install --upgrade pip
```

1.2 Basic Usage of pip

Now that you've got `pip` installed, let's learn how to use it. Think of `pip` as your personal shopper for Python packages. You tell it what you want, and it goes to the Python Package Index (PyPI) supermarket to fetch it for you.

- **Installing a Package:**
  To install a package, just type the following:

```
pip install <package-name>
```

  For example, to get the magical `requests` library that makes HTTP requests as easy as pie (or should we say "Python's `pi`"?), you'd type

```
pip install requests
```

- **Listing Installed Packages:**
  Want to see what you've already installed? Just type the following:

```
pip list
```

  It will list all the packages in your Python environment.

- **Upgrading a Package:**
  Python packages evolve faster than a chameleon at a disco. To upgrade a package, use

```
pip install --upgrade <package-name>
```

For instance, to bump your HTTP requests module up to date and groovy, run the following:

```
pip install --upgrade requests
```

1.3 Managing Python Packages with pip

Now that you're equipped with the basics, let's get a bit more adventurous. Picture this: you're building a space rocket (because why not?), and it needs a rocket dashboard filled with widgets and doodads. Each widget is a Python package, and you need to manage them.

- **Freeze Your Environment:**
  Ever wanted to capture the exact state of your Python environment for later? To create a list of installed packages, use:

```
pip freeze > requirements.txt
```

It's like taking a snapshot of your spaceship's dashboard.

- **Install from Requirements:**
  Need to recreate that exact environment on another spaceship (or computer)? To install all the packages listed in your requirements file, use:

```
pip install -r requirements.txt
```

- **Uninstalling Packages:**
  If a package is causing trouble or you just don't need it anymore, you can say goodbye with the following command (Don't worry; it won't hold a grudge):

```
pip uninstall <package-name>
```

- **Searching for Packages:**
  Sometimes you know what you want, but you're not sure if it exists. No problem! The below command will help you find packages that match your query:

```
pip search <search-term>
```

1.4 Benefits

- Widely used and a standard for Python package management.
- Simple to use and great for most Python projects.
- Large package repository on PyPI.
- Easy integration with other tools and IDEs.

1.5 Cons

- Doesn't handle non-Python dependencies.
- Dependency management can sometimes be less strict.

1.6 Uniqueness

- While it's the most common package manager, it primarily focuses on Python packages and doesn't handle non-Python dependencies.

So there you have it, folks! The essentials & fundamentals of `pip`. It's your Python package passport to the stars, and with it, you'll be exploring & adventuring through Python's universe of packages in no time. In the following chapter, we'll step into the world of virtual environments and learn how to keep our packages from having epic battles over who gets to control Python.

Chapter 2: Virtual Environments: Packages Playground

Ahoy, Python pioneers! In this chapter, we're taking a delightful detour into the fascinating world of virtual environments. Think of them as those magical closets in children's stories that lead to hidden lands. In this case, the land is a neatly organized, isolated Python environment.

2.1 What Are Virtual Environments?

Picture this: You're hosting a grand party (a Python project, of course) and want to invite a bunch of different characters (Python packages). Now, you don't want these characters causing chaos, getting into fights, or messing up your party (read: conflicting with each other). This is where virtual environments come to the rescue.

- **Virtual Environments Defined:**
  A virtual environment is like a secret chamber where you create a pristine, isolated Python environment. Inside this chamber, you can install packages, and they won't interfere with packages installed in other chambers. Think of it as having separate party rooms for your guests.
- **Why We Need Them:**
  Imagine you're working on two Python projects, "SpamClassifier" and "CatRecognizer." SpamClassifier relies on Python 3.7, while CatRecognizer insists on Python 3.9. If they were guests at your party, they'd argue about the dress code all night! Virtual environments ensure each project gets the Python version it desires, avoiding conflicts and chaos. Virtual environments keep the peace, allowing you to have multiple Python environments on your system, each with its own set of packages.

2.2 Using venv (Python 3.3+)

Let's start with the built-in tool that Python provides for creating virtual environments: venv. It's like a DIY costume shop for your Python projects.

- **Creating a Virtual Environment:**
  To create a virtual environment using venv, open your terminal and navigate to your project folder. Then run the following command:

```
python -m venv env_name
```

  where env_name is the name you want for your virtual environment.

- **Activating the Environment:**
  Imagine you've built this fantastic treehouse, and you want to hang out in it. To activate a virtual environment, you just need to "climb up" into it.

```
# On windows, use the below command
<environment-name>\Scripts\activate

# on Linux/Mac, use the below command
source <environment-name>/bin/activate
```

Above command would activate the virtual environment and now, when you're inside, your Python commands will use this environment's packages.

- **Deactivating the Environment:**
  Eventually, you'll want to come back to the real world (or at least your system's default Python environment). To deactivate, simply type

```
deactivate
```

This will take you back to your regular Python environment.

- **Installing Packages Inside the Environment:**
  While you're in your cozy virtual environment, use pip to install packages as you normally would. They'll be confined to this environment and won't spill over into your system's Python.
- **Exiting the Environment:**
  When you're done with your virtual adventure, don't forget to deactivate it. Think of it as leaving the treehouse after a fun day of playing Pythonic games.

2.3 Using virtualenv (Python 2.x and 3.x)

Not everyone has upgraded to Python 3.3 or later, so let's talk about virtualenv. It's like the trusty old treehouse you've had for years.

- **Install virtualenv:**
  If you haven't already, install virtualenv globally by running:

```
pip install virtualenv
```

- **Creating a Virtual Environment:**
  To create a virtual environment with virtualenv, simply type

```
virtualenv <environment-name>
```

It's like building your treehouse wherever you want.

14

- **Activating the Environment:**
  This process is similar to the `venv` activation.

```
# On windows, use the below command
<environment-name>\Scripts\activate

# on Linux/Mac, use the below command
source <environment-name>/bin/activate
```

- **Deactivating the Environment:**
  Whether you're in a virtual treehouse or a virtual cabin, you can always leave by typing the following:

```
deactivate
```

  It's the universal exit door.

- **Installing Packages and More:**
  Inside your virtual environment, you can use `pip` to install packages, just like in the `venv`. But `virtualenv` also has some additional features and options for advanced users.
- **Exiting the Environment:**
  As with `venv`, it's good etiquette to deactivate your environment when you're done. You don't want to be that person who leaves their treehouse door wide open.

2.4 Isolating Project Dependencies

Think of your virtual environment as your project's dressing room. When you invite a new package to your project, it can try on various outfits (versions) without affecting your other projects. If it doesn't fit, you can politely ask it to leave without causing a commotion in your Python party.

In essence, virtual environments ensure that your Python projects play nice with others and don't throw a tantrum when it comes to Python versions or package dependencies. It's like hosting a costume party where every guest gets to wear their favorite attire without quarreling over who gets the fanciest hat.

So, there you have it, folks! Virtual environments are like the secret chambers of the Python world, allowing you to keep your packages organized, happy, and far away from package conflicts. In the next chapter, we'll explore a tool that streamlines Python project management and makes package handling even more delightful. It's called Pipenv, and it's your ticket to Pythonic paradise!

Chapter 3: Pipenv: Streamlining Project Management

Ahoy, Python craftspersons! It's time to put on your dancing shoes and boogie down with Pipenv. Think of Pipenv as the Python package management tool that not only gets the party started but also ensures that your packages don't crash into each other like clumsy dancers on a crowded dance floor.

3.1 Introduction to Pipenv

Picture this: You're hosting a grand ball on your spaceship (you sure do love space parties), and you need to make sure everything runs smoothly. You need a bouncer to check invitations, a DJ to keep the beats going, and a mixologist to serve up cosmic cocktails. Pipenv is your all-in-one event planner for Python projects!

Pipenv combines `pip` (the package installer) and `virtualenv` (the isolation chamber) into a single, elegant tool. It's like having a party coordinator who takes care of the guest list, the entertainment, and even makes sure the decorations match your spaceship's interior.

3.2 Installing and Setting Up Pipenv

To kick off the party with Pipenv, you'll need to install it first. Remember, this isn't just any package manager; it's a party planner for your Python project!

1. **Install Pipenv:**
   Open your terminal or command prompt and simply run

```
pip install pipenv
```

Pipenv is your Python party genie, and this is how you summon it. You may also use `brew` in Mac for installing `pipenv`, use the following alternative with `brew` (we will cover brew in later chapters):

```
brew install pipenv
```

2. **Create a New Project Folder:**
   Let's say you're hosting a disco party for space explorers. Create a new folder for your project, like `space-disco`.
3. **Navigate to Your Project Folder:**
   Use `cd space-disco` to enter your project's universe.
4. **Initialize a Pipenv Environment:**
   Now, for the grand reveal! Type the following command,

```
pipenv install
```

Pipenv will create a magical Pipfile and a Pipfile.lock that keep track of your Python dependencies. It's like having a guest list with RSVPs. If you want to specify a specific python version, you can also run,

```
pipenv install --python 3.x
```

where `3.x` is the Python version you want to use.

5. **Activate the Pipenv Shell:**
   And now, you're about to enter inside the cozy Pipenv party room. Your Python project will be in its own happy space after activation. Let's get things activated by running the following command,

```
pipenv shell
```

3.3 Creating and Managing Pipenv Projects

With Pipenv in charge, managing your Python packages becomes as easy as picking the perfect party playlist.

- **Adding Packages:**
  Need to invite a new guest (new package) to your party (your project)? Use the following command to add packages to your Pipfile:

```
pipenv install <package-name>
```

- **Listing Packages:**
  Wondering who's on your guest list? The following will show you all the packages and versions you've invited.

```
pipenv requirements
```

- **Removing Packages:**
  If someone's not grooving to the beat, send them home with

```
pipenv uninstall <package-name>
```

Imagine your space disco. You have got neon lights, funky beats, and dancers in zero-gravity

3.4 Locking Dependency Versions

Imagine your space disco. You have got neon lights, funky beats, and dancers in zero-gravity suits. Now, imagine someone suddenly and unexpectedly swapping out the neon lights for disco balls. Chaos, right? That's what happens when package versions change unexpectedly.

Pipenv keeps your party decorations consistent by locking down your package versions. When you run

```
pipenv lock
```

This generates a Pipfile.lock that specifies the exact versions of all your packages. No surprises, just smooth dancing.

3.5 Using Pipfile and Pipfile.lock

Your Pipfile is like the DJ's playlist; it tells Pipenv which packages to install. The Pipfile.lock, on the other hand, is the DJ's mixing board, ensuring that the versions match perfectly.

- **Pipfile:**
  You can edit this file manually if you want to tweak your package choices. Think of it as your DJ's request list.
- **Pipfile.lock:**
  Leave this file alone! Pipenv takes care of it for you, making sure your packages stay in sync with what's on the Pipfile.

3.6 Collaboration and Sharing Projects

You've thrown an amazing space disco party with Pipenv, and now your fellow space explorers want to join in. Here's how you can share the fun:

- **Sharing Your Pipfile:**
  Share your Pipfile with others so they know which packages to install. It's like sending them the party playlist.
- **Lock in the Fun:**
  Don't forget to include your Pipfile.lock! It ensures that everyone's dancing to the same beat. In pythonic terms, it makes sure the packages are consistent for everyone's use
- **Installation Magic:**
  Your friends can recreate your party with a simple command (if the Pipfile and Pipfile.lock is consistent)

```
pipenv install
```

It's like teleporting them to your space disco.

3.7 Pipenv for Development and Deployment

Pipenv isn't just about throwing epic Python parties; it's also handy for development and deployment:

- **Development Dependencies:**
  You can specify development-only dependencies by using

```
pipenv install --dev package-name
```

These are like the backstage crew at your party, making sure everything runs smoothly behind the scenes.

- **Deployment:**
  Pipenv ensures that your deployed environment matches your development environment, making deployment as smooth as a well-choreographed dance routine.
- **Environment Cleanup:**
  When the party's over, clean up the virtual environment using,

```
pipenv --rm
```

This leaves your project folder tidy and ready for the next shindig.

3.8 Custom Scripts and More

Pipenv isn't just about managing dependencies; it's your party planner, DJ, and security all rolled into one. Here are a few more tricks up its sequined sleeve:

- **Running Custom Scripts:**
  Sometimes you need to run custom Python scripts as part of your project. Pipenv allows you to do this with ease. Just create a [scripts] section in your Pipfile and define your custom scripts there. For example:

```
[scripts]
my_script = "python my_script.py"
```

You can then execute your script with

```
pipenv run my_script
```

Checking for Security Vulnerabilities:
Worried about uninvited guests (security vulnerabilities) crashing your party? Pipenv has a built-in solution for this. To check for security vulnerabilities in your project's dependencies, run the following command:

```
pipenv check
```

Locking Python Version:

You can specify a particular Python version for your project using the [requires] section in your Pipfile. For example:

```
[requires]
python_version = "3.8"
```

- This ensures that everyone joining your project knows which Python version to bring to the party.

Sample of complete Piplock file:

```
[[source]]
url = "https://pypi.org/simple"
verify_ssl = true
name = "pypi"

[packages]
requests = "*"
flask = "==2.0.0"
numpy = { version = "*", markers = "python_version >= '3.6'" }

[script]
test = "pytest --cov"

[dev-packages]
pytest = "*"

[requires]
python_version = "3.9"
```

Let's break down its sections with some brief information:

[[source]]: This section defines the package source repository from where Pipenv should fetch packages. The name attribute typically identifies the repository (e.g., "pypi" for the Python Package Index).

[packages]: This section lists the project's main dependencies along with their version constraints. Dependencies defined here are essential for the project to run correctly.

[dev-packages]: Similar to [packages], this section lists development-only dependencies. These are packages used during development, testing, or debugging.

[requires]: This section specifies the Python version required for the project. It helps ensure that everyone working on the project uses a compatible Python version.

[script]: This section is where you can define some custom scripts that Pipenv can execute within your project's virtual environment.

So there you have it, Python Craftspersons! Pipenv is the ultimate Python project manager, making sure your packages dance together harmoniously and without stepping on each other's toes. In the next chapter, we'll explore Poetry, the modern maestro of Python packaging. Stay tuned for more Python party tips!

Chapter 4: Poetry: Python Packaging with a Touch of Elegance

Ahoy there, Python pioneers! Welcome to Chapter 4, where we're about to embark on a poetic journey into the heart of Python packaging with Poetry. It's like the Shakespeare of package management—elegant, lyrical, and occasionally prone to dramatic twists!

4.1 Introducing Poetry

Ahaa! Here comes my favorite Package manager, Poetry. Before we dive into the nitty-gritty of Poetry, let's set the stage. Imagine you're planning an epic intergalactic party, and you want everything to be perfect. Poetry is your party planner, decorator, and bouncer all rolled into one.

But why should you choose Poetry for your Python projects? Well, let's see:

- **Dependency Management:** Poetry manages your project's dependencies and versions effortlessly. It ensures that everyone is on the same page, like a book club that always discusses the same edition.
- **Package Management:** Creating Python packages is a breeze with Poetry. It assembles your project's code, dependencies, and metadata into a beautiful package, ready for distribution.
- **Publication Made Easy:** Poetry simplifies the process of publishing your packages to PyPI (Python Package Index) or other repositories. It's like sending your poetry to the world with just a click.

4.2 Installing Poetry

To start using Poetry, you need to invite it to your project. Don't worry; it won't eat all the cake. Just follow these simple steps:

1. **Install Poetry:**
   Open your terminal and run

```
pip install poetry
```

   Think of it as sending an elegant invitation to Poetry.

2. **Initialize Your Project:**
   There are two ways to achieve this. You can use the following command:

```
poetry new <project-name>
```

This would create a directory with name `<project-name>` and also necessary files to start your Python epic.

Now the other way is to manually create and navigate to your project folder and run

```
poetry init
```

Poetry will guide you through creating a `pyproject.toml` file, which is like your party plan for Python packages.

4.3 Managing Dependencies with Poetry

Now that Poetry is your party planner, let's see how it manages dependencies with a touch of poetic flair.

- **Adding Dependencies:**
  To add a package to your project, use `poetry add <package-name>`. It's like inviting a character to join your Python play. For example:

```
poetry add requests
```

- **Adding Dev Dependencies:** Just as actors rehearse backstage, you can add development dependencies with `poetry add --dev <package-name>`.These are tools and libraries needed during development or testing. For example:

```
poetry add -dev pytest
```

- **Removing Dependencies:**
  If a character becomes unruly, you can bid them farewell with `poetry remove <package-name>`. No more dramatic exits!

```
poetry remove requests
```

- **Updating Dependencies:**
  Keep the party fresh by updating packages:

```
poetry update
```

- **Generating a Lock File**
  Just like a stanza in a poem, Poetry generates a `poetry.lock` file to lock down your dependencies. This is similar to the working and purpose of lock file used in `pipenv` To

ensures that your project uses specific package versions, run

```
poetry lock
```

4.4 Poetry Project and config Structure

A Poetry project is as organized as a librarian's secret bookshelf. Here's how it's structured:

- `pyproject.toml`: Your project's centerpiece. It's a TOML file where you define dependencies, Python version, and other project settings. Think of it as your project's manuscript.
- `poetry.lock`: Similar to Pipenv's `Pipfile.lock`, this file locks down precise dependency versions. It's your project's poetry anthology.
- `src/`: The directory where your Python source code lives. Think of it as the stage where your Python actors perform.
- `tests/`: Where your tests reside. Every good story needs a bit of drama, right?

Find the basic directory structuring below,

```
poetry_app
├── poetry.lock
├── pyproject.toml
├── README.md
├── src
│       └── __init__.py
└── tests
        └── __init__.py
```

4.5 Poetry's `pyproject.toml` File

Poetry's `pyproject.toml` file is where the magic happens. It's like your project's script for a blockbuster movie. Here's a taste of what it looks like:

```
[build-system]
requires = ["poetry-core>=1.0.0"]
build-backend = "poetry.core.masonry.api"

[tool.poetry]
name = "my-python-party"
version = "0.1.0"
description = "An epic Python party project"
```

```
authors = ["Your Name <your.email@example.com>"]

[tool.poetry.scripts]
greet = "my_module:main"

[dependencies]
python = "^3.9"
requests = "^2.26.0"
flask = "^2.0.0"

[dev-dependencies]
pytest = "^7.0.0"
```

- `[tool.poetry]`: This section contains project-specific details, like the project's name, version, and author. It's the guest list for your Python packages.
- `[tool.poetry.scripts]`: This section holds custom scripts which you want to define. The above `pyproject.toml` file, creates a script called `greet` that calls the `main` function from `my_module.py`. And to run the custom scripts,

```
poetry run <script-name>
```

And from the above example, to run the `greet` script,

```
poetry run greet
```

- `[dependencies]`: Here, you list the packages your project needs to run, along with their versions. Poetry uses this to set up your party.
- `[dev-dependencies]`: These are packages you need for development or testing, like a DJ for your party. Poetry keeps them separate from the main dependencies.

4.6 Publishing Your Poetry

Every poet dreams of sharing their work with the world. With Poetry, publishing your package on PyPI (Python Package Index) is as easy as reciting a sonnet.

1. **Packaging Your Poem:**
   Create a distributable package by generating a `.tar.gz` file in the `dist` directory using the following command:

```
poetry build
```

2. **Publishing on PyPI:**
   Upload your masterpiece to PyPI with command - `poetry publish`. Follow the prompts to enter your PyPI credentials and share your poetry with the world.

```
poetry publish
```

4.7 Poetry in Action: An Example

Let's create a simple Python project using Poetry. Imagine we're writing a Python script to greet the world with a humorous message. Here's how we can do it:

1. **Initialize a New Poetry Project:**

```
poetry new greetings
cd greetings
```

2. **Edit `pyproject.toml` to Add Dependencies:**
   Open `pyproject.toml` and add the `requests` library:

```
[tool.poetry.dependencies]
python = "^3.8"
requests = "^2.26.0"
```

3. **Define a Script:**
   Create a Python file named `greet.py` inside the `src/` directory:

```python
import requests

def main():
    response = requests.get("https://icanhazdadjoke.com/",
headers={"Accept": "text/plain"})
    print(response.text)
```

4. **Define a Script Entry in `pyproject.toml`:**
   Open `pyproject.toml` and add the following under `[tool.poetry.scripts]`:

```
[tool.poetry.scripts]
greet = "greet:main"
```

5. **Run the Script:**
   Execute the `greet` script:

```
poetry run greet
```

Now you've created a Python project using Poetry that fetches a dad joke from a website and greets the world with humor.

Poetry, with its poetic approach to project management, simplifies Python packaging and dependency management. It's your trusted companion in crafting Python masterpieces. In the next chapter, we'll explore more Pythonic wonders that will leave you awestruck. Until then, keep writing and keep coding!

Chapter 5: Conda: Managing Complex Environments and Beyond

Greetings, Pythonistas! In this chapter, we set sail on the high seas of Python environment management with a tool that's as versatile as a Swiss Army knife — Conda.

5.1 What is Conda?

Picture Conda as the shipbuilder of your Python armada. It's not just about managing Python environments; it's about creating entire fleets of them. Conda is a cross-platform package manager and environment management system.

5.2 Installing Conda

To get Conda on board, follow these steps:

1. **Download Conda:**
   Visit the official Conda website and grab the installer for your platform. It's like recruiting a new crew member for your ship.
2. **Install Conda:**
   Run the installer and let Conda take its place on your ship. It's a smooth process, much like setting up a hammock on the deck.
3. **Check Installation:**
   Open your terminal and type `conda --version` to make sure Conda is on board. You should see its version number. Consider it a friendly "Greetings!" from Conda. But don't stop there and check for additional information using `conda info`

```
conda info
```

5.3 Managing Environments with Conda

Imagine you're sailing to different islands, each with its own set of supplies. You wouldn't want to mix up the coconuts with the pineapples, would you? Conda lets you create separate environments for your Python projects, just like isolated islands for each adventure.

Creating an Environment:

To create a new environment, use `conda create --name myenv`. You've just claimed a new island, `myenv` ! You can also set the python version as well for this environment. The below command creates an environment named myenv with Python 3.9 installed.

```
conda create --name myenv python=3.9
```

Creating an Environment for a Specific Platform:

You can specify the platform when creating an environment. For example, to create an environment for macOS, use:

```
conda create --name myenv --platform darwin
```

Creating an Environment File:

Use `conda list --export > environment.yml` to create an environment file named `environment.yml`. It's like documenting your quest.

```
conda list --export > environment.yml
```

Recreating the Environment:

To recreate the environment from the environment file, run:

```
conda env create -f environment.yml
```

Activating an Environment:

Navigate to your environment with `conda activate myenv`. It's like stepping onto your newly claimed island.

```
conda deactivate
```

Deactivating an Environment:

When you're done exploring your island, use `conda deactivate` to return to your main ship.

```
conda deactivate
```

5.4 Managing Packages with Conda

Conda can not only create environments but also stock them with supplies (Python packages) for your adventures.

Installing Packages:

To install packages in your environment, use `conda install <package-name>`. It's like restocking your island with coconuts and pineapples. Below is an example for installing two packages - `numpy, matplotlib`

```
conda install numpy matplotlib
```

Listing Installed Packages:

Check your island's inventory with command - `conda list`. It's like taking stock of your supplies.

```
conda list
```

Update Packages:

To ensure your treasures are up to date, use `conda update <package-name>`. For example:

```
conda update pandas
```

Removing Installed Packages:

If you find moldy coconuts, remove them with `conda remove <package-name>`. Keep your island fresh and clean!

```
conda remove matplotlib
```

5.5 Exploring Conda Channels

In Conda, channels are like secret maps to hidden treasures (packages). By default, Conda uses the main channel (like the Pirate Bay of packages), but there are many others to explore.

Adding Channels:

To add a channel, use `conda config --add channels <channel-name>`. It's like charting a new course to a different treasure island.

```
conda config --add channels conda-forge
```

Conda Forge is like a bustling marketplace for Python packages, where you can find treasures galore.

Finding Packages:

Search for packages in a channel with `conda search <package-name>`. It's like scanning the beach for buried treasure chests.

```
conda search pandas
```

5.6 Conda as a Universal Soldier

Conda isn't limited to Python—it's a versatile warrior in the world of data science and beyond. It can manage packages and environments for languages like R, Julia, and more.

Managing Non-Python Packages:

With Conda, you can easily manage packages for other languages. For example, for R packages:

```
conda install -c r r-essentials
```

5.7 Conda Environments in Action: An Example

Let's set sail on a Python adventure with Conda. Imagine we're exploring a mysterious island where we need to calculate the circumference of coconut trees. Here's how we can do it:

Create a Conda Environment:

```
conda create --name coconut-island python=3.11
```

Activate the Environment:

```
conda activate coconut-island
```

Install Necessary Packages:

```
conda install numpy matplotlib
```

Write Python Script:

Create a Python script, `coconut_circumference.py`, to calculate the circumference:

```python
import numpy as np
import matplotlib.pyplot as plt

# setting some random diameter
tree_diameters = np.random.randint(10, 30, 100)
```

```python
# circumference = pi * diameter
tree_circumferences = np.pi * tree_diameters

plt.hist(tree_circumferences, bins=20)
plt.xlabel('Circumference (cm)')
plt.ylabel('Frequency')
plt.title('Coconut Tree Circumference Distribution')
plt.show()
```

Run Python Script:

```
python coconut_circumference.py
```

Now you've embarked on a Python adventure to the coconut island, complete with your Conda environment and packages. It's like being the captain of your Python ship, exploring uncharted domains and territories.

Conda's flexibility and versatility make it an astounding choice for managing complex Python environments, whether you're exploring islands, solving mysteries, or just having some Python fun. In the next chapter, we'll unveil more Pythonic wonders to keep you entertained on your programming journey. So, hoist the sails, and let's set course for new horizons!

Chapter 6: Pixi: Where Python Packages Meet Pure Magic!

Ahoy, Pythonistas! In this chapter, we are going to explore a young and recently built magic wand — Pixi,.to swing around to manage environments and packages.

6.1 Hello Pixi !!

Pixi is a fast package manager, inspired from Cargo of Rust, built using Rust on top of the existing conda ecosystem. With Pixi, managing software packages becomes a breeze and the platform boundaries are broken down. It can help to produce reproducible environments across operating systems without Docker by automating lockfiles. Pixi supports Python, R, C/C++, Rust, Ruby, and more. As far as I know, this is the youngest package manager with a fast growing community.

Why Pixi ?!

- **Reproducible:** Work in dedicated, isolated reproducible environments
- **Clean & Intuitive User Interface:** User-friendly design reduces the learning curve & and makes it a joy to work with.
- **Multi-platform support:** Ensure compatibility across Windows, MacOS, and Linux.
- **Robust Dependency Management:** Easy to add, remove, or update packages in your project and automatically handles version conflicts.

6.2 Pixi Installation

Open the terminal and use commands of any of the below methods to trigger pixi installation in the machine.

1. Using Pip

```
pip install pixi
```

2. Using cURL & bash

```
curl -fsSL https://pixi.sh/install.sh | bash
```

3. Using `brew`

```
Brew install pixi
```

6.3 Pixi Project

There are two ways to achieve this using pixi. You can use the following command:

1. Creating & initializing new Project

```
pixi init <project-name>
```

This would create a directory with name `<project-name>` and also a file named `pixi.toml`. To make sure to setup Python project, add python using pixi.

```
pixi add python
```

2. Initializing existing projection in a directory.

Navigate to your project folder and run

```
pixi init
```

The same `pixi init` command can be used in combination with different arguments to suit our purpose

The `pixi.toml` is the pixi project configuration file, or should we say the project manifest

Find the basic directory structuring below,

```
pixi_app
├── pixi.lock
├── pixi.toml
├── README.md
├── src
│     └── __init__.py
└── tests
       └── __init__.py
```

- **`pixi.toml`:** Similar to poetry's `pyproject.toml`, this is the project's centerpiece. All the dependencies, Python version, and other project settings are defined in this TOML file. Additionally, one can also mention the **channels** from which the packages are fetched. In other words, it is the artifact repository. It may also be an absolute path in the filesystem..

- **pixi.lock:** Similar to poetry's `poetry.lock`, this file locks down precise dependency versions.
- **src/:** The directory where your Python source code lives.
- **tests/:** Where your tests reside. Every good story needs a bit of drama, right?

6.4 Managing Pixi Package Dependencies

Now, let's see how our pixi dust could handle the dependencies.

1. To add dependencies to the TOML file, use the command `pixi add <package-name>`. The notable part, is that.the specified package is added only when its version constraint is able to work with rest of the dependencies in the project. Here is the example of the command:

```
pixi add requests
```

2. To have more control over Dependencies, pixi provides many argument options over `pixi add` to enable projects to have multiple levels of environments and their dependencies - standard dependencies (run deps), host dependencies, build dependencies, pypi dependencies, and even platform dependencies

```
pixi add --host "python>=3.11.0"
pixi add --build cmake
pixi add --pypi requests
pixi add --platform osx-64 --build clang
```

3. To install the dependencies from the existing lock file

```
pixi install
```

4. To search for a package and get the latest version of the package, use the command `pixi search <package-name>`. For example,

```
pixi search requests
```

5. To publish the package one can build the package and then use the upload command `pixi upload <HOST> <PACKAGE_FILE>` to push the package to the channel.

```
pixi upload repo.prefix.dev/my_channel my_package.conda
```

6.4 Pixi Configuration file Structure

Pixi uses the `pixi.toml` file for holding the configuration, dependencies and other information. Here is a glimpse of how it looks like:

```
[project]
name = "my-pixi-python-party"
version = "0.1.0"
description = "An epic Python party project"
authors = ["Your Name <your.email@example.com>"]
Channels = ["conda-forge", "nvidia"]
platforms = ["osx-arm64", "osx-64", "win-64"]
license = "MIT"
readme = "README.md"

[system-requirements]
unix = true
macos = "11.0"

[tasks]
greet = "python -c 'print(\"hello\")'"

[activation]
scripts = ["env_setup.sh"]

[dependencies]
requests = ">=2.31.0,<2.32"

[host-dependencies]
python = ">=3.11.0"

[build-dependencies]
cmake = ">=3.28.1,<3.29"

# To support windows platforms as well add the following
[target.win-64.activation]
scripts = ["env_setup.bat"]

[target.osx-64.build-dependencies]
clang = ">=17.0.6,<17.1"
```

- [project]: This holds the project metadata, as in, the information about the project. This includes, and not limited to, name, version, description, authors, license, list of platforms that the project supports, list of artifact repository that defines the channels used to fetch the packages from. Pixi solves the dependencies for all these platforms and puts them in the lockfile.

- **[tasks]**: In Pixi, tasks are a way to automate custom commands in the project. For example, a `lint` or `format` command. As noticeable, this is the same as the custom scripts in `pipenv` and `poetry`. One more valuable feature is that one task can be set as a dependency of another task and thereby, serializing the execution of the tasks. New tasks can be added either by manually entering it into the TOML file or using the command `pixi task add <TASK_NAME> <CUSTOM_COMMAND>`. If there is need to add a dependency task, use `--depends-on` argument. Here is an example for adding a task to run `ls` command with current working directory as `tests`:

```
pixi task add tls ls --cwd tests
```

To run the task use `pixi run <TASK_NAME>` command

```
pixi run tls
```

- **[system-requirements]**: This section is to mention the minimal system specifications which will be used while resolving dependencies. The above mentioned file holds the default system requirement for `osx-arm64` platform.
- **[activation]**: This section holds a list of scripts that will be sourced when the environment is activated while running `pixi run` or `pixi shell` commands. As per the example configuration file above, the script `env_setup.sh` is run whenever the environment is activated.
- **[dependencies]**: This section holds all the list of packages that are installed into the environment. In other words, these are run time dependencies.
- **[host-dependencies]**: This section holds the dependency list that are only needed while building the project but no longer needed after installation of the project. Simple example would be Base Interpreters - a Python package need `python` and an R package need `mro-base` or `r-base`
- **[build-dependencies]**: This holds the dependencies that are needed to build the project. But unlike the other dependency categories mentioned before, these dependencies are installed for the architecture of the build machine. The build target refers to the machine that will execute the build. For example, `cmake` is used in build machine while compiling the project.

  Quoting from the official documentation, here is an example to distinguish and understand the build & host dependencies. If you compile on a MacBook with an Apple Silicon chip but target Linux x86_64 then your *build* platform is `osx-arm64` and your *host* platform is `linux-64`.

- **[target.<PLATFORM>.<CONF>]**: This can help in defining configurations specific to the platform like tasks, dependencies, activation specific to the platform. Here are few examples,
  `[target.win-64.activation]` means activation configuration specific for `win-64` platform
  `[target.osx-64.tasks]` means tasks configuration specific for `osx-64` platform

`[target.linux-64.build-dependencies]` means build dependencies configuration specific for `linux-64` platform

Although the learning curve for Pixi is a little bit steep compared to other python package managers, recently I have grown interested with this package manager..

Chapter 7: Advanced Package Management

Welcome, intrepid Python adventurers! In this chapter, we're going to explore advanced package management techniques that will take your Python journey to the next level. Get ready for a wild ride!

7.1 Managing Multiple Python Versions with pyenv

Imagine you're a Python enthusiast with a collection of vintage Python versions, like rare wine bottles. Meet pyenv, your Python cellar manager.

Installation and Basic Usage

First, you'll need to install pyenv. It's as easy as ordering pizza:

```
# On macOS using Homebrew
brew install pyenv

# OR

# For a quick installation
curl https://pyenv.run | bash
```

Managing Python Versions:

- List available Python versions: `pyenv install --list`
- Install a specific Python version: `pyenv install 3.9.7`
- Set a global Python version: `pyenv global 3.9.7`

Python Virtual Environments:

Pyenv can also manage virtual environments with the `pyenv-virtualenv` plugin:

```
# Install the plugin
brew install pyenv-virtualenv

# Create a virtual environment
```

```
pyenv virtualenv 3.8.6 myenv

# Activate the virtual environment
pyenv activate myenv
```

Now, you're juggling Python versions like a pro! ☐

7.2 Isolating Python Versions with Miniconda

Do you need a minimalist approach to managing Python environments? Miniconda is like a tiny spaceship for Python, giving you precise control. Miniconda is more like a minimal installer version of Conda which we explored in the previous chapter.

Installing Miniconda:

You can acquire your own Miniconda terrarium from the official website - https://docs.conda.io/en/latest/miniconda.html

Creating a New Environment:

With Miniconda, you can create isolated Python environments for your projects:

```
conda create --name myenv python=3.9
conda activate myenv
```

It's like having your own mini-biosphere for Python!

7.3 Using Homebrew on macOS

macOS users, rejoice! Homebrew is your magical elixir for installing and managing Python and other packages. Well, not just python, it's more of a tools and package manager for the entire macOS

Installing Homebrew:

To install Homebrew, use the following one-liner:

```
/bin/bash -c "$(curl -fsSL
https://raw.githubusercontent.com/Homebrew/install/HEAD/install.sh)"
```

Installing Python with Homebrew:

With Homebrew, installing Python is a breeze:

```
brew install python@3.9
```

Now, you can sip on your freshly brewed Python, straight from the keg!

7.4 Package Management on Linux Distributions

For the Linux explorers, package management varies depending on your distribution. Let's try installing python on different linux flavours:

Debian/Ubuntu (apt):

```
sudo apt install python3.10
```

Red Hat/Fedora (dnf):

```
sudo dnf install python3.10
```

Arch Linux (pacman):

```
sudo pacman -S python
```

Now you can enjoy Python with the taste of your favorite Linux flavor!

7.5 Managing Python-Based Command-Line Tools with pipx

Ever wished your Python tools acted like superheroes? Pipx is here to grant your command-line tools superpowers!

Installation and Usage of pipx:

To install `pipx`, run:

```
pip install pipx
```

Now, you can install command-line tools in isolated environments. For example, lets try installing the tool `black` :

```
pipx install black
```

And run the tool `black` without conflicts:

```
black --help
```

Your command-line tools are now unstoppable!

7.6 Best Practices and Tips for Package Management

Now that you've journeyed through various package management tools and techniques, here are some best practices and tips to keep in mind:

- **Use Virtual Environments:** Always use virtual environments to isolate project dependencies.
- **Document Your Environment:** Keep an environment file (e.g., `requirements.txt` or `pipfile` or `environment.yml`) to document project dependencies.
- **Regularly Update Packages:** Keep your packages up-to-date to benefit from bug fixes and new features.
- **Back Up Your Environment:** Backup your environment files to recreate your working environment if needed.
- **Version Control:** Use version control systems like Git to track changes in your code and environment files.
- **Stay Informed:** Stay updated on Python and package releases to make informed choices about dependencies.
- **Clean Up Old Environments:** Periodically remove old or unused virtual environments to free up space.
- **Hit Home Run:** Don't be afraid to explore new tools and techniques. Python package management is a vast playground

Congratulations, Python explorer! You've now become a package management maestro. Armed with these advanced techniques, you're ready to conquer Python's wild frontiers. Keep coding, and may your Python adventures continue to be exciting and fun!

Chapter 8: Case Studies

8.1 Real-Time Case Studies

Case Study 1: Web Scraping with Beautiful Soup

Scenario: You're building a web scraper to fetch the latest news headlines from a news website.

Tool: Pipenv

Example:

1. Create a Pipenv environment for your project:

```
pipenv install requests beautifulsoup4
```

2. Write a Python script `scraping.py` to scrape the data from a website:

```python
import requests
from bs4 import BeautifulSoup

url = 'https://www.thehindu.com'

# Send an HTTP GET request
response = requests.get(url)

# Check if the request was successful
if response.status_code == 200:
    # Parse the HTML content of the page
    soup = BeautifulSoup(response.text, 'html.parser')

    # Extract specific data from the page
    title = soup.title.string
    print(f"Title: {title}")
```

```
    # Extract headlines
    for i, headline in enumerate(soup.find_all('h1')):
        print(f"headline {i + 1}: {headline.text}")

    # Extract Paragraph
    for i, paragraph in enumerate(soup.find_all('p')):
        print(f"Paragraph {i + 1}: {paragraph.text}")

else:
    print("Failed to retrieve the page.")
```

3. To run this code, use the below command

```
pipenv run python scraping.py

# or first activate the virtual env and then run the script
pipenv shell
python scraping.py
```

Outcome: Your Python script now scrapes and displays the latest news headlines, keeping you informed in style!

Case Study 2: Scientific Computing with SciPy

Scenario: You're conducting scientific experiments and need to perform complex mathematical calculations.

Tool: Conda

Example:

1. Create a Conda environment for your scientific project

```
conda create --name sci-computations python=3.11
conda activate sci-computations
conda install scipy numpy matplotlib
```

2. Write a Python script (computations.py) to perform advanced mathematical calculations:

```
import numpy as np
from scipy.optimize import curve_fit
import matplotlib.pyplot as plt
```

```
# Your scientific calculations go here

x = np.linspace(0, 10, 100)
y = 2 * x + 1 + np.random.normal(0, 1, 100)  # Simulated data with noise

def linear_func(x, a, b): # setting up a linear function for the problem
    return a * x + b

params, covariance = curve_fit(linear_func, x, y)
a, b = params

# Plot the data and the fitted line
plt.scatter(x, y, label='Data')
plt.plot(x, linear_func(x, a, b), 'r', label='Fitted line')
plt.legend()
plt.show()
```

Outcome: With Conda, you have a dedicated environment for your scientific experiments, and your Python script performs complex mathematical calculations and displays the results beautifully.

8.2 Data Science and Machine Learning with Anaconda

Case Study: Sentiment Analysis (Anaconda)

Scenario: You're working on a sentiment analysis project using scikit-learn and NLTK. Sentiment analysis involves analyzing text data to determine the sentiment or emotional tone expressed in the text, such as positive, negative, or neutral sentiments.

1. Create an Anaconda Environment

The first step is to create an isolated environment using Anaconda. This environment will contain all the necessary packages for your sentiment analysis project.

```
conda create --name sentiment-analysis python=3.9
conda activate sentiment-analysis
```

Here, we've created an environment named "sentiment-analysis" with Python 3.9 as the interpreter.

2. Install Required Packages

Next, you need to install the required packages for your sentiment analysis project. In this case, you'll need scikit-learn and NLTK.

```
conda install scikit-learn nltk
```

Scikit-learn is a powerful machine learning library, and NLTK (Natural Language Toolkit) provides tools for working with human language data.

3. Write the Sentiment Analysis Script

Now, let's write a Python script (`sentiment.py`) to perform sentiment analysis on text data. This script uses NLTK's VADER (Valence Aware Dictionary and sEntiment Reasoner) sentiment analysis tool, which is specifically designed for analyzing sentiment in text.

```python
import nltk
from nltk.sentiment.vader import SentimentIntensityAnalyzer

nltk.download('vader_lexicon')

def analyze_sentiment(text):
    sid = SentimentIntensityAnalyzer()
    sentiment = sid.polarity_scores(text)
    return sentiment

if __name__ == "__main__":
    text = "I love this product! It's amazing."
    sentiment = analyze_sentiment(text)
    print(sentiment)
```

In this script:

- We import the necessary libraries, including NLTK and the SentimentIntensityAnalyzer.
- We download the VADER lexicon, which is used for sentiment analysis.
- We define a function `analyze_sentiment` that takes a text input and returns sentiment scores.
- We analyze a sample text, "I love this product! It's amazing," and print the sentiment scores.

Step 4: Run the Sentiment Analysis Script

Now, you can run the sentiment analysis script:

```
python sentiment.py
```

The output will show sentiment scores for the provided text, including positive, negative, neutral, and compound scores.

This demonstrates how Anaconda can be used to create an isolated environment for data science and machine learning projects, allowing you to manage dependencies efficiently. Sentiment analysis is a valuable application in various fields, including customer feedback analysis, social media monitoring, and more.

8.3 Web Development

Case Study: Building an Weather API with FastAPI (Poetry)

Scenario: You're creating a modern API using FastAPI to provide weather information.

1. **Create a FastAPI project using Poetry:**

```
poetry new weather-api
cd weather-api
poetry add fastapi uvicorn
```

2. **Write your FastAPI application (**main.py**):**

```python
from fastapi import FastAPI

app = FastAPI()

@app.get("/")
def read_root():
    return {"Hello": "Weather API"}

@app.get("/weather/{city}")
def get_weather(city: str):
    # In a real application, you'd fetch weather data here.
    return {"City": city, "Weather": "Sunny"}
```

3. **Run your FastAPI app:**

```
poetry run uvicorn main:app --reload

# OR alternatively, you can also setup poetry scripts
```

Your FastAPI-powered weather API is up and running! You can access it at the domain http://localhost:8000 in your browser or via API requests.

Case Study: Building a Blog with Flask (pipenv)

Scenario: You're building a simple blog using Flask to share your coding adventures and manage dependencies using pipenv

1. **Create a Flask project using Pipenv:**

```
pipenv --python 3.11
pipenv install Flask
```

2. **Write your Flask application (**app.py**):**

```python
from flask import Flask, render_template

app = Flask(__name__)

@app.route('/')
def home():
    return render_template('home.html')

if __name__ == '__main__':
    app.run(debug=True)
```

3. **Set up your HTML template (**templates/home.html**):**

```html
<!DOCTYPE html>
<html>
<head>
    <title>My Coding Adventures Blog</title>
</head>
<body>
    <h1>Welcome to My Coding Adventures Blog!</h1>
    <p>Stay tuned for exciting coding stories!</p>
</body>
</html>
```

Note: Flask internally uses Jinja package for template rendering

4. **Run your Flask app:**

```
pipenv run flask run

# OR
pipenv shell
flask run

# OR you can set custom pipenv scripts for this purpose
```

Your Flask blog is live at `http://localhost:5000`. Share your coding adventures with the world! ☐☐

These case studies demonstrate how to set up web applications using FastAPI with Poetry and Flask with Pipenv. FastAPI offers a modern and fast API development experience, while Flask provides a straightforward path to creating web applications. Whether you choose FastAPI or Flask depends on your project's requirements, but with the right package management tool, you're all set to embark on your web development journey! ☐☐

8.4 Managing Cross-Platform Applications with Conda

Case Study: Cross-Platform Game (Conda)

Scenario: You're developing a cross-platform game using Pygame

Tool: Conda

1. Create a Conda environment for your game:

```
conda create --name mygame python=3.7
conda activate mygame
conda install pygame
```

2. Write your Pygame-based game (game.py):

```
import pygame
pygame.init()

screen = pygame.display.set_mode((400, 300))
pygame.display.set_caption("Cross-Platform Game")

running = True
while running:  # run indefinitely
    keys = pygame.key.get_pressed()
    if keys[pygame.K_SPACE]:
        pygame.quit()  # Quit when spacebar is pressed
```

3. Run the game

```
python gampe.py
```

Your simple game is now ready for cross-platform players everywhere!

8.5 Command-Line Tool Distribution with pipx

Case Study: Markdown Converter (pipx)

Scenario: You've developed a command-line tool named "markdown-converter" that converts Markdown files to HTML. You want to distribute it to make it easily accessible to other users.

1. Developing Your Markdown Converter Tool

Before distributing your tool, you need to develop it. Here's a simple Python script for the Markdown converter (`converter.py`):

```python
import sys
import markdown

def convert_markdown_to_html(input_file, output_file):
    """
    converts markdown file content into html file content
    """
    with open(input_file, 'r') as md_file:
    markdown_text = md_file.read()
    html_text = markdown.markdown(markdown_text)

    with open(output_file, 'w') as html_file:
    html_file.write(html_text)

if __name__ == "__main__":
    if len(sys.argv) != 3:
        print("Usage: converter.py input.md output.html")
        sys.exit(0)
    input_file = sys.argv[1]
    output_file = sys.argv[2]
    convert_markdown_to_html(input_file, output_file)
    print ("Conversion completed !")
```

This script takes two arguments: the input Markdown file and the output HTML file.

2. Creating a Python Package

To distribute your tool, you should organize it as a Python package. Create a directory for your package and add your converter script inside it. For example:

```
markdown_converter
├──── README.md
```

```
├── converter.py
├── setup.py
└── __init__.py
```

3. Preparing the Package for Distribution

You'll need to create a setup.py file to describe your package and its dependencies. Here's a minimal setup.py for your markdown-converter package:

```python
from setuptools import setup

setup(
    name='markdown-converter',
    version='1.0',
    py_modules=['converter'],
    install_requires=[
        'markdown',
    ],
    entry_points='''
        [console_scripts]
        markdown-converter=converter:main
    ''',
)
```

In this setup.py:

- name is the name of your package.
- version specifies the package version.
- py_modules lists the Python modules to include (in this case, just 'converter').
- install_requires lists the package's dependencies (e.g., 'markdown').
- entry_points defines a console script entry point, which allows you to run your tool from the command line as "markdown-converter."

This minimal setup can help in building the package and its necessary dependencies

4. Building and Distributing the Package

To build your package for distribution, use the following commands:

```
pip install setuptools wheel
python setup.py sdist bdist_wheel
```

This will create a "dist" directory with distribution files.

5. Installing Your Tool Locally

Before distributing your tool with `pipx`, you can install and test it locally to ensure everything works as expected. Navigate to the "dist" directory and run:

```
pip install .
```

6. Distributing Your Tool with pipx

Now, it's time to distribute your tool using `pipx`. First, you need to publish your package to the Python Package Index (PyPI). You can use a service like `twine` to do this:

```
pip install twine
twine upload dist/*
```

After publishing, users can install and use your tool with `pipx`:

```
pipx install markdown-converter
```

Once installed, users can run your tool from the command line:

```
markdown-converter input.md output.html
```

Your Markdown converter tool is now easily accessible to others, allowing them to convert Markdown files to HTML effortlessly! □➡□□

Chapter 9: Troubleshooting & Best Practices

Welcome to the world of Python package management, where adventure and occasional hiccups go hand in hand. In this chapter, we'll explore how to troubleshoot common issues and follow best practices to ensure your Python projects sail smoothly

9.1 Common Issues and Their Solutions

Issue 1: Dependency Hell

The Problem: Dependency conflicts can turn your Python project into a battlefield, where incompatible package versions clash, causing errors and chaos.

The Solution: The power of isolated environments with `pipenv` or `poetry` comes to the rescue. These tools create a virtual environment for your project, keeping dependencies separate and under control.

Using `pipenv`:

1. Change to your project directory.
2. Run `pipenv install` to create a virtual environment and install dependencies from your `Pipfile`.

Using `poetry`:

1. Navigate to your project directory.
2. Run `poetry install` to create a virtual environment and install dependencies from your `pyproject.toml`.

By isolating your project's dependencies, you'll bid farewell to dependency conflicts.

Issue 2: Mysterious Import Errors

The Problem: You encounter the dreaded "ModuleNotFoundError" when trying to import a package, leaving you scratching your head.

The Solution: Here are a few steps to unravel this mystery:

- Ensure your virtual environment is activated. If you're using `pipenv` or `poetry`, activate it with `pipenv shell` or `poetry shell`.

- Double-check that you've installed the required package. If not, use `pipenv install your_package` or `poetry add your_package` to install it.

By following these steps, you'll banish those import errors to the shadows.

Issue 3: Python Version Woes

The Problem: You need to work on projects with different Python versions, but managing them becomes a headache.

The Solution: Enter `pyenv`, your Python version management wizard. Here's how to wield its power:

1. Install the desired Python version using `pyenv install`, e.g., `pyenv install 3.11`.
2. Set the global Python version with `pyenv global`, e.g., `pyenv global 3.9`

Now, you can effortlessly switch between Python versions like a true Python sorcerer.

Issue 4: Inconsistent Environments

The Problem: Your development environment differs from your colleague's, causing discrepancies in package versions and behaviors.

The Solution: Achieve environment consistency by using environment files. Different tools offer different files:

- `requirements.txt`: Standard for `pip` and `virtualenv`.
- `Pipfile.lock`: Used by `pipenv` for deterministic installations.
- `pyproject.toml`: The choice for `poetry` users.

These files capture your dependencies and their versions, ensuring everyone dances to the same Python tune.

Issue 5: Slow Package Downloads

The Problem: Slow package downloads can hinder your workflow, making you feel like you're waiting for a snail-mail owl.

The Solution: Consider using a different package source or mirror. Some options include:

- Using a regional mirror for faster downloads.
- Specifying a custom package index URL using `--index-url`.
- Utilizing a package manager like `pipenv` or `poetry` that allows you to set custom mirrors in their respective configuration files.

By optimizing your package download strategy, you'll escape the clutches of sluggish downloads.

With these solutions in your arsenal, you're better equipped to tackle common issues in Python package management. Embrace your inner Python wizard, and may your code be bug-free and your dependencies harmonious! ☐☐

9.2 Ensuring Reproducible Environments

In the enchanting world of Python package management, reproducibility is akin to having a magic spell that ensures your software works the same way every time, no matter where it's run. It's a crucial aspect of software development, allowing you to recreate your development environment with precision, even if the original setup is lost to the mists of time. Let's delve deeper into ensuring reproducible environments and the tools that make it possible.

The Challenge of Reproducibility

Imagine you've crafted a marvelous Python project, complete with a host of dependencies. It works flawlessly on your machine. However, when you share it with a colleague or deploy it on a different machine, it fails mysteriously. What could have gone wrong? This is where the need for reproducibility arises.

Reproducibility ensures that anyone, anywhere, can recreate the same development environment and achieve identical results. It's the difference between waving a wand and hoping for the best versus casting a well-documented and precise spell.

Tools for Reproducible Environments

1. `requirements.txt`

The humble `requirements.txt` file is a classic way to specify dependencies and their versions. It's a plain text file listing the packages your project depends on. You can generate it by running:

```
pip freeze > requirements.txt
```

Others can recreate your environment using this file:

```
pip install -r requirements.txt
```

However, it doesn't capture everything, such as the Python version or non-Python dependencies.

2. `Pipenv` and `Pipfile.lock`

If you're looking for a more comprehensive solution, `Pipenv` comes to the rescue. It combines `pip` and `virtualenv` functionality while also managing your dependencies in a `Pipfile`. To ensure full reproducibility, you can create a `Pipfile.lock` file:

```
pipenv lock
```

This file contains precise version information for your dependencies, including transitive dependencies, python version, etc., ensuring an exact environment replica.

3. `Poetry` **and** `pyproject.toml`

For those who desire modernity and sophistication, `Poetry` is an excellent choice. It uses a `pyproject.toml` file, which not only lists dependencies but also defines your project's metadata and settings. To lock your environment:

```
poetry lock
```

The resulting `pyproject.lock` file contains comprehensive dependency information.

Why Reproducibility Matters

Reproducibility is essential for various reasons:

1. **Collaboration**: When working with a team, everyone needs to be on the same page. A reproducible environment ensures everyone uses identical dependencies and configurations.
2. **Continuous Integration**: Reproducible environments are crucial for CI/CD pipelines. They guarantee that your tests and builds run consistently.
3. **Deployment**: When deploying your application to different servers or platforms, reproducibility ensures that it behaves as expected everywhere.
4. **Debugging and Issue Resolution**: When issues arise, having a reproducible environment allows others to reproduce the problem easily and find solutions.
5. **Documentation**: Reproducibility is a cornerstone of good project documentation. It ensures that newcomers can set up the project without a hitch.

Best Practices

Here are some best practices to enhance reproducibility:

- **Use Version Constraints**: Specify version constraints in your dependency files to prevent unexpected updates.
- **Commit Dependency Files**: Commit your `requirements.txt`, `Pipfile.lock`, or `pyproject.lock` to version control. This guarantees that your project's dependencies are always available.
- **Use Virtual Environments**: Always work within a virtual environment to isolate your project's dependencies from the system Python.
- **Document Installation Steps**: Provide clear installation instructions for your project, including the commands to recreate the environment.
- **Regularly Update Dependencies**: Periodically update your project's dependencies to include security patches and improvements. Remember to test thoroughly after updates.
- **Automate Environment Creation**: Use scripts or automation tools to create the development environment automatically, reducing the chances of manual errors.

Reproducibility is like a magic wand that ensures your Python spells (code) perform consistently across different platforms and environments. By following best practices and using the right tools, you can craft code that is both magical and reliable.

9.3 Security Considerations

In the ever-evolving landscape of software development, security is not a charm you cast once and forget about; it's an ongoing vigilance. To safeguard your Python projects against potential vulnerabilities, consider the following:

1. **Regularly Update Packages:**

Just like wizards need to update their spells to stay powerful, your Python packages require updates to stay secure. Use `pip` or `poetry` to upgrade packages:

```
# Using pip
pip install --upgrade your_package

# Using poetry
poetry update
```

2. **Security Scanners:**

You don't need a crystal ball to foresee potential security threats; you have security scanners! Tools like `safety` can help identify known vulnerabilities in your project's dependencies:

```
# Using safety
safety check
```

Additionally, you can use `bandit` to scan your Python code for common security issues:

```
# Using bandit
bandit -r your_project_directory
```

These are Software Composition Analysis (SCA) tools - Websites like the National Vulnerability Database (NVD) and the Common Vulnerabilities and Exposures (CVE) system are like the Oracle of our world, offering insights into potential threats.

3. **Dependency Auditing:**

When you are adding a new package into the project; you'd want to verify them. SWith `pipenv` and `poetry`, you can check the security of your project's dependencies:

```
# Using pipenv
pipenv check

# Using poetry
```

```
poetry check
```

These commands inspect your project's dependencies for known security vulnerabilities and provide guidance on how to address them. Infact, `pipenv` uses `safety` in the background for this purpose.

4. Version Pinning:

Lock down your dependencies to specific versions in your `Pipfile`, `Pipfile.lock`, or `pyproject.toml` to prevent unintended upgrades that might introduce vulnerabilities.

5. Maintain Virtual Fortress

Virtual environments are like the magical fortresses of our project. They provide isolation and ensure that spells (packages) used in one project don't interfere with spells in another. Always create a virtual environment for your project. Tools including `pipenv`, `poetry`, `venv`, etc., helps in setting up a secluded virtual environment.

6. Monitor Security Advisories:

Stay informed about security advisories related to the packages you use. Many projects maintain a security mailing list or publish advisories on their websites. Keeping an eye on these can help you react promptly to any security warnings.

7. Continuous Integration (CI):

Integrate security checks into your CI/CD pipelines. Services like GitHub Actions, Travis CI, or Jenkins can automatically run security scans and tests whenever you push code.

8. Prune Unused Dependencies:

As a wise wizard once said, "Keep only what you need." Regularly review and prune unused or unnecessary dependencies from your project to minimize potential attack surfaces.

9. Trusted Sources:

Always fetch packages from trusted sources. PyPI (the Python Package Index) is the official repository for Python packages. Beware of third-party sources and verify their integrity.

Remember, security in the world of software development is an ongoing journey, not a one-time spell. By following these practices and using tools like `pipenv`, `poetry`, and security scanners, you can help protect your Python projects from the dark arts of cyber threats. Stay vigilant, and may your code always be secure! ⬜⬜⬜

9.4 Keeping Dependencies Up to Date

Ah, the dance of the packages! The packages evolve over time, sometimes bringing new powers (features) and squashing old bugs. It's essential to keep them up to date for a robust and secure application. Here's how you can ensure your packages are on the latest version:

1. **Update a Single Package:**

Use `pip` to update a specific package to its latest version:

```
pip install --upgrade your_package
```

Replace `your_package` with the actual package name you wish to update.

2. **Update All Packages:**

To update all packages in your environment, you can use `pip` with a little bit of Python magic:

```
pip freeze | sed -ne 's/==.*//p' | xargs -n1 pip install -U
```

This command retrieves a list of installed packages, removes the version numbers, and then updates each package.

3. **Update Packages in requirements.txt:**

If you have a `requirements.txt` file, you can update all packages listed to their latest versions:

```
pip freeze --local | grep -v '^\-e' | cut -d = -f 1  | xargs -n1 pip install -U
```

This command reads your `requirements.txt`, finds the installed packages, and updates them.

4. **Update Packages with `poetry`:**

If you're using `poetry`, it simplifies updating all packages in your project:

```
poetry update
```

5. **Update Packages with `pipenv`:**

If you're using `pipenv`, it simplifies updating all packages in your project:

```
pipenv update
```

This command reads your `Pipfile`, finds the latest compatible versions for your packages, and updates them accordingly.

Remember, with great power (of updated packages) comes great responsibility. Always ensure that updates won't break any existing functionality in your application. You can do this by having thorough tests and considering the changes in each update.

Updating your packages regularly keeps your projects secure, efficient, and aligned with the ever-evolving Python ecosystem. Stay updated, and may your Python craftworks always be in harmony with the latest magic!

9.5 Cleaning Up and Managing Disk Space

In the world of Python package management, it's easy to accumulate a multitude of packages and their various versions. Over time, this can consume a significant amount of disk space on your system. To maintain a tidy and efficient development environment, it's essential to know how to clean up and manage disk space effectively. Let's explore some key techniques and tools to achieve this:

1. Remove Unused Packages:

The first step in decluttering is to identify and remove packages that you no longer need. Python's `pip` comes to the rescue with the `autoremove` command:

```
pip autoremove
```

This command analyzes your environment and identifies packages that are no longer required by any installed package. It then gracefully removes them, freeing up space.

2. Clear Cache Files:

Python stores cached files and build artifacts that can accumulate over time. These files are typically found in the `__pycache__` directories and may include compiled Python files (`.pyc`), which are no longer needed once you're done with a project. Use the following command to sweep them away:

```
python -m py_compile -b
```

3. Delete Old Virtual Environments:

If you're using virtual environments to isolate your Python projects (a recommended practice), you might forget to clean them up after you're done. To list your virtual environments using `venv`:

```
python -m venv list
```

Then, remove the ones you no longer need:

```
python -m venv remove <environment_name>
```

4. Manage Package Cache:

`pip` caches downloaded packages to avoid redownloading them in the future. However, this cache can grow over time. You can limit the size of this cache by using the `--no-cache-dir` flag when installing packages:

```
pip install --no-cache-dir your_package
```

And additionally, you can periodically clear the cache manually:

```
pip cache purge
```

5. Check Disk Usage:

You can use system monitoring tools to keep an eye on your disk space usage. Tools like `du` (disk usage) and graphical applications can help you identify directories that are consuming the most space:

```
du -h --max-depth=1 /path/to/directory
```

This command will display a summary of disk usage for your Python packages, helping you identify which environments are consuming the most space.

6. Monitor Disk Space:

Always keep an eye on your system's available disk space. Tools like `df` on Linux or macOS and the built-in storage management on Windows can help you stay informed about your system's overall disk usage.

7. Automating Cleanup:

To maintain a clean environment regularly, you can schedule cleanup tasks as part of your system maintenance. Create a simple script that runs the `pip autoremove` and cache purge commands, and then schedule it to run periodically using cron (on Unix-like systems) or Task Scheduler (on Windows).

By regularly performing these cleaning and management tasks, you can maintain a tidy and efficient Python environment, ensuring that you have ample space for your code crafting adventures. Remember, a clutter-free workspace is the secret to Developer's peace of mind!

Conclusion

Ah, what a journey it's been! Welcome to the grand finale of this epic adventure through the realm of Python package management! As you bid adieu, let's do a brief recap of our journey

Recap of Key Takeaways

In our magical journey, we discovered an array of spells and wands (tools) to manage our Python packages. From the classic `pip` to the modern `Poetry`, and the versatile `Conda`, each tool has its own charm. So now, the key takeaway? Choose wisely, for the right tool can make your Python adventures a breeze!

Choosing the Right Tool for Your Projects

Always remember to choose your tool wisely for your further python exploration:

- For web development, consider **Pipenv** or **Poetry** or **Pixi** for Flask, FastAPI or Django projects.
- In data science and machine learning, embrace **Anaconda** for its data magic.
- For command-line tools, wield **pipx** to distribute your creations far and wide.
- When developing cross-platform applications, trust **Conda** or **Pixi** to ensure harmony across systems.
- Use **pyenv** for version control when working on projects with specific Python requirements.
- Opt for **Miniconda** if you desire a minimalistic Conda experience. But personally, I would still suggest on using **Pixi** for this similar cases considering its implementations, features and its flexibility
- On macOS, let **Homebrew** simplify your Python package management journey.
- For system-level packages on Linux distributions, native package managers are your allies.
- When working on isolated scripts or custom packages, explore **Pipenv** or **Poetry** or **Pixi**.

Embracing Best Practices

To become a true Python package management wizard, remember these best practices:

- **Isolation**: Always use virtual environments or isolated environments for your projects.
- **Dependency Management**: Keep dependencies well-documented and pinned to specific versions.

- **Security**: Regularly update packages and use tools like `safety` to scan for vulnerabilities.
- **Reproducibility**: Use environment files (e.g., `requirements.txt`, `Pipfile.lock`, or `pyproject.toml`) for reproducible environments.
- **Cleanup**: Regularly clean up unused packages and cached files to free up disk space.

Future of Python Package Management

Python package management is constantly evolving to meet the needs of developers. Several trends and advancements are shaping the future of Python package management to add support for Cloud integrated, streamlined dependency management, isolation and containerisation, improved caching, enhanced security measures, etc. Here are few such package managing tools:

- `huak` (https://github.com/cnpryer/huak)

This is a rust based package manager with fantastic developer onboarding experience. Although this is WIP (Work In Progress), it aims at providing resilient speed.

- `Flit` (https://github.com/pypa/flit)

Flit is a lightweight and simple package manager for Python. It focuses on building and distributing packages with minimal configuration. Flit integrates well with modern Python packaging tools and supports features like PEP 517/518 for building packages.

- `Hatch` (https://hatch.pypa.io)

This is a package manager and project generator for Python. It aims to simplify the process of creating and managing Python projects by providing a streamlined workflow. Hatch includes features like dependency management, virtual environments, and project templates.

- `Spack` (https://spack.readthedocs.io)

Spack, a simple package manager, designed to support multiple versions and a wide variety of platforms and environments. In other words, installing a new version of a dependency does not break existing installations, so many configurations can coexist on the same system – happily non-destructive package manager.

- `PDM` (https://spack.readthedocs.io)

PDM is a modern python package manager that helps in boosting the development workflow in many aspects. Unlike other notable package managers, it doesn't need to create a virtual environment at all to install and manage packages in the project. PDM's community is growing out well, thanks to 's support for custom plugin development by the users.

- `Rye` (https://rye-up.com)

Although `Rye` is still an experimental python package manager, it could still help developers for almost all their pythonic needs.The best part about this package manager is that It supports monorepos and global tool installations. This is, just like `Pixi`, also inspired by `rustup` and `cargo` from `Rust`

Your Journey as a Python Package Manager Master

Congratulations! You've completed your apprenticeship in the art of Python package management. You're now a full-fledged master of Python Package Manager.

Remember, your journey doesn't end here. The world of Python is vast, and there are countless tools and packages to discover. Keep exploring, keep coding, and keep spreading the magic of Python.

Now, go forth, pythonistas, and may your code always run swiftly, your dependencies stay secure, and your Pythonic adventures be ever enchanting!

Appendix A: Quick Reference Guides

Welcome to the treasure trove of quick references and cheat sheets! In this appendix, we've compiled essential cheat sheets for various Python package management tools like Pip, Pipenv, Poetry, Conda, and more. Plus, we've conjured up a handy glossary to decode the mystifying jargon of the Python package management realm. Let's dive in!

Cheat Sheets for Pip, Pipenv, Poetry, Conda, and Other Tools

1. Pip Cheat Sheet

Pip is your trusty Python package manager, but it's always good to have a quick reference handy:

```
pip install package_name         # Install a Python package
pip uninstall package_name       # Uninstall a Python package
pip freeze                       # List installed packages
pip search package_name          # Search for a package
pip show package_name            # Show package information
pip install --upgrade package_name  # Upgrade a package
pip install -r requirements.txt # Install packages from a requirements file
```

2. Pipenv Cheat Sheet

Pipenv is like the wizard's staff of package management. Here's your quick guide:

```
pipenv install                   # Create a virtual environment and install
dependencies
pipenv shell                     # Activate the virtual environment
pipenv install package_name      # Install a package and update Pipfile
pipenv lock                      # Generate a lock file (Pipfile.lock)
pipenv uninstall package_name    # Uninstall a package
pipenv --rm                      # Remove the virtual environment
```

3. Poetry Cheat Sheet

Poetry is your all-in-one Python packaging solution. Here's your cheat sheet:

```
poetry new project_name          # Create a new Python project
poetry add package_name          # Add a package to your project
poetry install                   # Install project dependencies
poetry build                     # Build the project package
poetry publish                   # Publish your package to PyPI
poetry run python script.py      # Run a Python script in the virtual
```

4. Conda Cheat Sheet

Conda is your versatile package manager. Here are some essential commands:

```
conda create --name env_name python=3.8   # Create a Conda environment
conda activate env_name                    # Activate the environment
conda install package_name                 # Install a package
conda list                                 # List installed packages
conda env list                             # List Conda environments
conda deactivate                          # Deactivate the current environment
conda remove --name env_name --all         # Remove an environment
```

5. Pipx Cheat Sheet

Pipx helps manage Python-based command-line tools. Here's your reference:

```
pipx install package_name     # Install a Python-based CLI tool
pipx upgrade package_name     # Upgrade a CLI tool
pipx uninstall package_name   # Uninstall a CLI tool
pipx list                     # List installed CLI tools
pipx run package_name         # Run a CLI tool in a temporary environment
```

6. Pixi Cheat Sheet

Fast, reliable & cross-platform supported Pixi are your command-line servie. Here's your reference:

```
pixi init project_name            # Initialize a Project
pixi install                      # Install dependencies from lock file
pixi info                         # Info overview of machine/project
pixi project channel add conda-forge   # Add new channel to project
pixi add package_name             # Install a package
pixi search package_name          # Search a package
pixi task add task_name command   # Add a pixi task for command
pixi run task_name                # Run a pixi task
pixi task remove task_name        # Removes a pixi task
pixi task alias task_name new_name  # Alias task name or concat tasks
pixi upload host package_file     # Upload a package to host
pixi auth logout host             # Logout of remote Host
pixi global install package_name  # Install package in system level env
pixi global remove package_name   # Uninstall package in system level env
```

```
pixi global list                    # List packages in system level env
pixi auth login host --token xxx    # Login to remote Host
```

Glossary of Terms

The magical world of Python package management is filled with mystical terms. Here's a glossary to help you decode them:

- **Package**: A collection of Python code and resources bundled together for distribution.
- **Dependency**: A package that your project relies on to function correctly.
- **Virtual Environment**: An isolated environment where Python packages can be installed independently of the system Python.
- **pipfile**: A configuration file used by Pipenv to manage dependencies.
- **pipfile.lock**: A lock file created by Pipenv to pin package versions for reproducibility.
- **Pixi.toml**: A configuration file used by Pixi to manage package information.
- **pixi.lock**: A lock file created by Pixi to pin package versions for reproducibility.
- **pyproject.toml**: A configuration file used by Poetry to manage package information.
- **poetry.lock**: A lock file created by Poetry to pin package versions for reproducibility.
- **Conda**: A cross-platform package manager used for installing and managing packages and environments.
- **Environment Variable**: A system variable that stores configuration information, often used to set paths for Python environments.
- **CLI Tool**: Command-line interface tool, often written in Python, used for specific tasks or utilities.
- **Repository (Repo)**: A central location where packages are stored and managed, like PyPI (Python Package Index), Conda-Forge, etc.
- **Dependency Hell**: The situation where conflicting dependencies make it difficult to install or run packages.
- **Security Scanner**: A tool that checks packages for known security vulnerabilities.
- **Lock File**: A file that records the specific versions of packages used in a project to ensure reproducibility.
- **Distribution**: A version of Python or a package that is distributed to users.
- **Cache**: Temporary storage used to speed up package installation and retrieval.

With these cheat sheets and glossaries at your disposal, you're well-prepared to navigate the enchanting world of Python package management. May your spells (commands) be effective, and may your Python projects flourish like well-nurtured magical creatures!

Appendix B: Additional Resources

In this appendix, we've compiled a list of recommended resources and advanced topics that will elevate your Python Expertise to a whole new level. Prepare to advance in your quest for pythonic wisdom!

Recommended Books, Websites, and Forums

Websites:

1. **python.org**: The motherland of Python! Find official documentation, tutorials, and all things Python here.
2. **realpython.com**: A treasure trove of tutorials and articles, catering to everyone from beginners to experts. Real Python, real good!
3. **stackoverflow.com**: The Oracle of Python wisdom. Got a question? Chances are, it's already been answered here.

Forums:

1. **reddit.com/r/python**: Python Reddit is a lively community of Python enthusiasts discussing everything from beginner questions to advanced Python concepts. The memes are a bonus!
2. **pythonweekly.com**: Your weekly dose of Python news, articles, and curated content delivered right to your inbox. A magical newsletter, indeed!

Advanced Topics for Further Learning

1. Machine Learning and AI:

Level up your Python spells and delve into the realms of machine learning and artificial intelligence. Unleash algorithms that predict the future (well, almost).

- **Libraries**: Explore scikit-learn, TensorFlow, PyTorch, and Keras.
- **Courses**: Complete Machine Learning & Data Science Bootcamp 2023 in udemy
- **Books**: "Hands-On Machine Learning with Scikit-Learn, Keras, and TensorFlow" by Aurélien Géron.

2. Web Development:

Become the master of web creation, crafting your digital castles and magic portals to the online world.

- **Frameworks**: Dive into Django, Flask, FastApi, etc. for Python-powered web development.
- **Courses**: The Complete 2023 Web Development Bootcamp on Udemy.
- **Books**: "Django for Beginners" by William S. Vincent, "Flask Web Development" by Miguel Grinberg and "Building Data Science Applications with FastAPI" by François Voron

3. Data Science and Visualization:

Unveil the secrets hidden in data. Be the Oracle of insights, revealing patterns and trends.

- **Libraries**: Learn about pandas, NumPy, Matplotlib, and Seaborn.
- **Courses**: "Data Scientist" Nano degree in Udacity
- **Books**: "Python for Data Analysis" by Wes McKinney.

4. Game Development:

Craft your own magical worlds, where you're the game master. Code your quests and slay the bugs!

- **Frameworks**: Explore Pygame, Panda3D, and Godot Engine.
- **Courses**: "Complete Python Game Development: From Scratch to Porting" on Udemy.
- **Books**: "Invent Your Own Computer Games with Python" by Al Sweigart.

Now, go forth, brave adventurer! Arm yourself with these resources, explore & dive deeper into Python, and level up your Expertise. Remember, every Python journey is a spellbinding adventure!

www.ingramcontent.com/pod-product-compliance
Lightning Source LLC
LaVergne TN
LVHW081804050326
832903LV00027B/2086